Cultivating the Divine

Healing the Dark Masculine

Book I

John Stone

Cover art by Judith Shaw:

Inanna in Her Boat of Heaven

For Carla and Mary, and the Countless Messengers in Spirit

Acknowledgements

A Special thanks to Judith for an amazing work of art, and to Erin, Nadine and Liz for invaluable help with editing...

Other Books by John Stone

Faeries Found, a guide to entering the Faerie Kingdom

Daring to Dream, a guide to Out of Body Travel

Future Books

Dream Trilogy, Books II and III

Contents

Preface

For those that are not familiar with my writing, I am a dream teacher—I help others reach higher states of conscious, to experience the dream and internal visionary world more lucidly, and to find that place where a deep oneness with all of life exists.

The guidance I find in these worlds inside of myself, where spirit teachers, guides and God can communicate with me, brings hope and inspiration to my life. And for me, that translates into a life lived with greater balance. This connection, I believe, is available for everyone but does require effort. Patience, practice and trust are needed to allow this presence to enter.

I don't often share visionary experiences in my writing, as I would prefer to show others how to have their own encounters with the Divine. But this book will include some of my out of body travels and lucid dreams, and how the knowledge I received was integrated into my life. Communicating with higher realms can be confusing for many reasons and I hope to show how one can interact with the world of spirit, while staying grounded in the physical realm. This is the first book in a Trilogy.

It seems in this age that many people aspiring to reach a higher consciousness become attached to feeling good and are often reluctant to face aspects of darkness inside of themselves. Others have already transmuted much of this element and have achieved an internal stability. But if you find yourself being thrown out of balance by the experiences in life, there is a reason. And discovering this element, what I call the *Dark Masculine*, can bring the greatest freedom. For as we purify our own darkness and learn to balance the masculine and feminine forces within, we are allowed to walk through doors of unrealized imagination and spiritual oneness.

It is in these moments that we may find inspiration from a Divine Source—through conscious dreams and highly spiritual visionary experiences…

Purification

Once honored as the primary force behind creation, feminine energy is not so well recognized today for its contributions in imagining and perpetuating our existence in the world. And the power of unseen energies from worlds beyond is easily forgotten when the overall consciousness drops to its more base, survival focused levels. But regardless of our unawareness of this power, it is still creating, calming, nurturing, and ever so delicately pulling us toward hope, balance and resolve. It is the primary stabilizing force in the Universe.

Yielding to desperation, the Divine Feminine overcomes the darkest moments, surviving until the next opportunity is presented. Wisdom knows that another opportunity for balance will be presented. Wisdom waits. Wisdom always waits for opportunity.

Entering the Dream World...

Deeply asleep and already dreaming, I saw several beings gathered around my body. Hovering slightly above me, their eyes were focused on a large kettle floating overhead. As it tipped toward me, I could see that it was filled with what seemed to be a gold liquid, a form of gold energy.

Pouring over me, I could feel it penetrating my skin, absorbing deeply into every cell of my body. As my body became saturated with the liquid, I felt a quickening, a rise in consciousness that I had never before known. Although still asleep, in just seconds I had shifted from experiencing this as a hazy dream, to being *fully conscious*—experiencing a consciousness that is far above this world. I had completely stepped out of the illusion of the Earth and had little awareness of my physical life, but I could now see through the darkness in the Earth. I no longer felt an alliance with what the people in the Earth had taught me about myself. *I was free.*

Releasing to the liberating and joyous frequencies of the higher dimensions, my awareness turned to those around me.

"We are so thankful for this meeting," A woman told me. "You had been attracting an accident to you that might have brought about your death."

The Gold energy had brought my body's vibration up to a frequency that was many levels above the Earth's consciousness. And my existence in this dimension prevented any negativity from reaching me. I could not even entertain a frightening thought here and I was able to *feel* knowledge that cannot be passed through words. As if an invisible Sanctuary was surrounding me, I could feel passages and corridors that could lead to ancient knowledge. I would only need to learn how to access them, doors that would soon reveal themselves to me during contemplation and meditation.

But the experience was not meant to last long. My body's level of purification would not allow it. This Gold energy had temporarily lifted my consciousness so that I could have a deep reminder of the other worlds, the work that was before me, and of the help waiting in the higher dimensions. I was very grateful for the meeting, though it did not leave my mind at rest…

*

I was at a time in my life when I had been experimenting with new forms of expression, initially focusing on art, drawing and painting. It seemed that this activity set up some form of magnetic connection to someone in the spirit world willing to help me learn more about the energetic forces within our world.

After falling soundly asleep, I found myself in the dream world, in a land somewhere in Europe. The time period seemed relevant to today, but the actual events did not relate to what the physical Earth was presently experiencing. And then…

I found myself in a village at the edge of town, in the art studio of Picasso.

Wide cobblestone pathways surrounded the studio on two sides, allowing the villagers to pass within sight of the painter as he worked. Large windows in the studio's stone walls opened the space to the public and his paintings were easily seen by anyone passing. It was a powerful view, uplifting.

But my time with him was not meant to be a mental experience. I was merely a witness, here to learn about his life in this community, to feel his feelings and to learn how to experience his level of detachment during violent times.

After several days, I became energetically divided between the beliefs of the surrounding village, and the focus of his work. While *he* was able to remain neutral to the building darker masculine forces, keeping his focus upon his own expression through painting, I felt a draw to what was happening outside. A war had broken out and many soldiers were passing by the studio daily.

It was as if I felt some obligation to help the others fight, and I had the urge to leave the studio and join them. All the while, Picasso effortlessly maintained his concentration on his life work, painting. If he was outside as soldiers passed, they didn't even seem to notice him. But they would gather around me, encouraging me to follow them to their meetings. I would disappear from Picasso's presence for hours, but I'd somehow make my way back and to observe and learn from him.

Here was a man, highly respected by the community, one that had no desire to be drawn into the physical violence of war. He felt compassion for me in the challenge I was facing, the compelling magnetic forces, but would never personally get caught up in the vibrations of the surrounding chaos. He remained peaceful, almost unaware of their existence.

I stayed with him a couple of weeks in Earth time, as I slowly began to release an attachment to violent thought. It was a very purifying period, as I was given the opportunity to choose between chaos and feeling the energy that flowed through him. I would come and go, but he would always be there when I returned, calmly painting away. My being was slowly releasing the darkness that was propelling me into conflict.

We had many conversations that helped me to evolve, but when I became more focused and able to receive the creative energies he was attuned with, I once asked,

"What was it like, when you finally reached the point when you could sell all of your paintings?"

"Well," he began. "You can't sell them all. But you paint, and you do well."

If this had been a simple dream, this statement might have not even been retained in my memory. But because it was a lucid experience, a state of consciousness where I experienced the feeling world many times over what I am able to feel in the awakened state, the energy behind the words shifted my consciousness. They had more power than simple words, as in dimensions beyond the third dimensional Earth, there are multiple aspects to every vibration. Air itself has a matter that can be molded, energetically sculpted to impact consciousness. And every action there has a greater effect. His words changed the vibration of my being, lifting my thoughts to a new level.

The gift of this experience was to show me how to suspend my own darkness, my own attachment to dark masculine thought. Instead of giving into passion, maintaining a connection with the mainstream thought in that land, I learned how to break that connection, but to do so without being attacked. I could see the acceptance and compassion that he had for those needing to be part of the violence—his lack of resistance to them *was* protection. This freed him to continue his work of bringing greater understanding through the unconscious realms.

*

When I have such powerful out of body and lucid dream experiences, I am changed from within. I can sometimes feel the difference for days as my body re-adjusts to the new level of consciousness. And as I ground the new consciousness, another dream experience arrives to offer further growth.

A common theme out of body experiences have is the power to impart knowledge into the body, in a way not paralleled by traditional learning. It is as if they change the molecular structure of the soul, causing one's thoughts to move through the mind in a different order, and at different levels of priority. What was once important might now pale in comparison to what seemed crucial before experiencing out of body travel. It's a change at soul level.

In reading about this, it sounds as though it is a miracle cure for many problems. And perhaps it is, with a catch. For when there are great internal changes, external changes are certain to follow. What someone once found interesting might no longer be appealing. And that means that all those in your life are also required to change, or at least adapt. So many prospective students might become afraid. The pressures felt from family and friends will prevent most people from allowing such dramatic life change.

*

While sleeping, I was talking to one of my teacher's guides, Mary, in a lucid out of body experience. She was telling me about a book that I could write, about a life interacting with her and my teacher, Carla Neff Gordan.

"You could show others how to learn in this way," She told me.

"I don't think I could write an entire book about it, because I don't actually see her that often," I replied.

At that point, the energy shifted as she slowly lifted her arm. Many images began appearing to her side, almost like browser windows on a computer, one cascading layer upon the other. Within each window was a memory of visiting with Carla—but memories that had never reached my consciousness. Memories of interacting with her in simultaneous, but unconscious dimensions and they were now instantly pouring into my mind.

"You can show people how to work with a Medium, how to live in the Earth while receiving guidance from above," She said.

The intensity of the energy did not permit me to stay in the experience much longer. But as I awoke, I wondered if this was a possibility.

Carla was a trance medium, meaning that she was a channel, but one that worked completely unconsciously—she could never remember a single word that she had ever spoken while in trance. And that made for some interesting expressions when I sometimes told her what she had said after she returned to consciousness. The being that spoke through her, called herself Mary.

In all the years I interacted with Mary, eleven in all, she never spoke much about herself. She did however say that she was not the mother of Jesus. And the only clue I ever heard about her prior life in Earth was once when she talked about India. She seems to have been some kind of Saint there, where she was cared for by others so that she could bless those visiting.

But Carla had an interesting life. Her unique ability to communicate with the worlds beyond began at age thirty-three. That is the year, as she says, she went into trance. It happened with her spiritual teacher, Helen. I don't remember exactly what they were attempting to do, perhaps just to meditate. But when Carla became conscious again a few hours later, thinking she had just been gone moments, her teacher told her what had happened. Quite moved, Helen showed Carla the notes she had been taking and told her that a being in the spirit world had been speaking through her all this time. Carla was stunned, but not completely convinced.

It hadn't been Mary that Carla initially channeled. It was another male spirit that was an interim conduit, until Carla's spiritual vibration was raised high enough to receive Mary.

But in the effort of convincing Carla that she was indeed speaking to those in higher realms, a miraculous event took place.

While she was in the trance state, the spirit told her of a local mortician that had made an unusual request of God. While preparing to bury a man, he placed a piece of paper in his lapel pocket, right before sealing the casket. On the paper was written something to the effect of, "If there really is a God, please give me evidence."

Well upon hearing this, Helen immediately wanted to visit the man and see if this was actually true. Carla was not so keen on the idea, but after some initial encouragement, and a promise that she wouldn't have to do any of the talking, she agreed to accompany Helen.

It apparently didn't take long to find the mortician and after confronting him with the story, to everyone's shock, he admitted that it was true. He also added that no one could have known, for he had told *no one*. All three were left stunned and Carla forced to face that her future had now changed…

Once in a conversation with Carla, and talking about my spiritual practice, she replied,

"Yes, right. Because I truly believe that you need a spiritual discipline as you are doing this. I went in through the new thought field. I was a psychologist but nobody was getting well that wasn't getting a spiritual experience. So I had studied for a long time, not meaning for it to go anywhere. But I just wanted to know for myself about 'new thought' (new age consciousness) because this hitting in me, that for me was like a review. And the guides have said that many people are in a review. They already know this ancient wisdom; they are just rethinking it into their current body, you know. The problems that you are learning you have known before where it's just a reminder," She finished.

Continuing our conversation, Carla explained how she began as a medium…

Because when I sat down and they starting telling me I would do this (referring to becoming a medium), I said to Helen, "Tell them I don't want to do this," She laughed.

"So they said they would give me a weekend to decide whether I wanted to do it or not. And after a lot of prayer, I said, "Ok, I would do that as long as I could be unconscious." I laughed out loud.

"And they have worked with me for the last 7 to 8 years trying to get me to try to be conscious and do it. But I'm sure I keep getting fearful and pulling away," She laughed.

"You know that is a problem with a lot of the channels, is the fear just keeps getting in the way. You see, Helen and I worked together for 18 months before we told anyone else what we were doing. So I worked alone with her. And she was my teacher, was my spiritual teacher, so I felt safe to do this with her. I was with her when it happened. And neither one of us had heard of this. We thought we invented a new thing for a while and then found out it had been going on forever," We both laughed.

"But sometimes accidents change our physical make up, you know. For instance I had a severe head injury when I was 2 ½ years old. I had one at 3 months too. I was in one of those jumper chairs and the spring broke and I went down on the soft spot and came within an ace of dying. But the guides said they were preparing the physical set up. You see? To (help me) do what I was going to do," She finished.

It would take me years to understand the importance of writing about my time with Carla. Besides just the fact that a conversation with Mary was awe inspiring, and more than a little ungrounding, many people had difficulty integrating the knowledge she shared into their physical lives. But through my own failures in understanding her messages, I began to see the difficulty of receiving information so directly from another realm. Her description of something that would occur in a month might actually translate into a wait of ten years. So it was very difficult to maintain a state of receiving, where I could be told of a future event and not remain attached to it. I never knew if an upcoming event would come to pass in a year, or a decade.

*

"It is joyful to be with yourself," Mary began in her distinctive accent. "You have a woman come today. White Buffalo Woman comes today to be a part of your initiation. Do you understand?"

"White Buffalo Calf Woman?" I asked in surprise.

"Yes, comes to the initiation. Because you, many of the guides who walk with you, are from the Native American walking. Do you see?" She asked.

"Uh huh," I replied.

"And one hold their totem towards you now to empower what you are going to do. That is why this such an important time because you are coming to your fullness. And in this age that you are now approaching quickly, this is going to lift you up so you can see great distance," She told me.

"One male that walk with you, his purpose with you—his name is *Great Thunder*. He is the power giver for you in your search. There are many things you have forgotten on your internal journey. But the information is there. But you don't remember in conscious mind. But when you are in need, it will be there for you to draw forth. You went on great journey, as you know under the Earth. And…"

"What just recently?" I asked, thinking she might be referring to my recent vision quest.

"Yes, yes. And in this journey you met with many ones who will meet again in the physical world that are to help you in your path. So you're not going off alone. There is also a male who work with you, who worked through another when they were in the Earth, White Eagle. This one comes today also to be witness for your acceptance. So everyone here for your acceptance," She laughed.

"So all you must do is accept what you have, to receive, to commit yourself to the changing of the Earth. And this simple thing. Yes? Very simple thing," She smiled.

"So many in the world are discouraged now. They believe there is no answer. And of course first step for them is to find internal peace. Because then you can hear—this for you also. Because as you are still, you can see great distance. When you are tense you block your own vision, you see, almost as though shoulders come cover your ears. But you have accomplished much that you do not yet realize. Much has already been done. So you are now ready for next step," She paused.

"So in your journey, in your writing. You must everyday write what you have learned in the day. And there will come a time when the poetry will flow from you again, and prose. This is very important."

"What is happening in your world, that which ones are frightened of…is undiscovered…unrevealed Love. So many years of your life, your love was pushed back into you. It was not drawn into the Earth, because of the fears of ones surrounding you. So that a part of your despair in early part of your life. Because it was almost as though you felt you could not be seen. And you felt almost as though, there was something defective, that ones could not see same as you. But you come with Universal vision, not the vision of Earth. So many of the things you have done, is to bring you knowledge of the Earth also. So your feet must be here, your head up here," She said, pointing first to the ground, and then to the sky.

"And you can do this," She laughed. "This better position than reversed."

"There is a young male not much different in age than you who comes today with great love for you. And to thank you for all that you gave. And his love for you very great," She paused.

"Is that Art?" I asked.

"Yes. And he says he stick around to see what you do with all this," We laughed.

"And your tenderness is what Earth need so much now. There was time you did not know you were tender and you tried to numb yourself so you would not be. But you see that you could not stay there. And the Earth reach you through your numbness and it says come back here."

"There is also a female here that gives you great love. And she says, 'There is so much she regrets.' She did not give that she could have. Same blood line as your own."

"My grandmother? I asked.

"Yes. And she said she could have given so much that she did not. But she said you come from a long line of stubborn people." We both laughed.

"But stubborn also, is consistency. You hold. You do not run away. When you truly see a vision, you will hold. And your vision is going to come clearer and clearer. Already you know what is in aura. You do not see, but you know what is there. So there is so much that you know that you do not realize you know because it does not come as big trumpet blaring. And you think this must not be much because this is so natural. *Of course this is natural.* This is your gift. Gifts always natural to the ones that have them."

"But even as a child small, you could already attune to others and know what they are feeling. You always could feel too much, is why you tried to hide, so you could not feel," She paused.

"Pray for the closeness to come. This is part of what you are going to end now, where you don't feel separate anymore. So that is *very* important. So you are in a journey of discovery. And it is *great* importance that you discover all these things you are searching for. So you will be both conscious and semi-conscious in your work. Though you will always be able to hear but not always understand what you are saying. Sometimes in the altered state you will hear words that come together but not perfectly. So you have to build between us a great trust."

"Recently I have been noticing I hear things in a deep state that don't seem to make any sense. Is that what's going on?" I asked.

"Yes, but they do make sense, but to you in altered state it is almost as though they are speaking in a foreign language, you see. So it does not make particular sense to you." She laughed.

"But it is full of sense," She added.

"You will find in your journey, that you will come to animals that you do not remember from this life. They are animals that have ceased their living long ago. Because you are going to go back into your different lives in order to pull the power from these. So you will see things and think, 'I believe that was a rumor only' and you will see that it is truth," She said.

"So I will see animals?

"Yes"

"Through my third eye?"

"Yes. And you will be in travel. In this travel you will see the unicorn, which did exist. Ones wanted it to be a magical thing but it was physically in the Earth. The myths are many true. But because those things no longer exist, ones believed they are make believe. But the magic is come back. The magic has come back. And you ones are going to do many magic things," She paused.

"If you will heal the mind of man, he will heal his own body. If you heal his body, he might hold the healing and he might not. Because you must change thought to do this. But many who were teachers to you in past time will come through your life in order to praise you, to encourage you, to go higher."

"In the spiritual realm?"

"Yes, and in the physical world. You will feel 'I have knowledge of them' because you have been with them before."

"When you are in Egypt and begin to take your class through initiation, your voice will guide them and keep them from fear. Many of those students will be back in your world for next step. So you're just in preparation. So you have to learn trust too. That is why we say to you so importance self love, because you have to trust. Large part of love is trusting. So you have to learn trust you."

"You have accomplished many things already. That is one thing we would like you to write in paper, how many things you have already accomplished. And you are still very young in years. So it will give you courage to say 'if I can do all of this, I can do the next thing also'."

"So what would you ask today?" She asked.

"Do my guides ever do anything in the physical to get my attention?"

"Yes, yes, often. And often they change things so you know they have been there. They want you to know that you are very well taken care of, so often they will move things around, for you to know that they are here."

"Is there anything I need to know about my childhood?" I asked.

"There were many things done to you that injured you. There are many things that you will recall when it is time to recall. Because what you need to know today, is that you ask that all things can be finished from the past."

"When I hear those high frequency sounds in my ears, what is that?" I asked.

"That is changing your hearing where we may speak to you directly."

"I am being spoken to in that moment?"

"No, we are repairing, we are fixing you where you *can* hear us. So we are making a different form of hearing, where you can hear both Earth and us."

"I hear that often," I added.

"Because we are working very diligently with you."

"When you were a child. Maybe 5, maybe 4 or 5. You believed you were Lone Wolf. You see? Wolf not alone. Wolf very family oriented. So what it is saying to you is Wolf is seeking its family back. So that is what you are going to learn in this life—that your family is scattered all over the Earth itself. And that you are going forth to find them. So here is piece of family here and piece of family here and here and you will bring them back together."

"You begin this journey in Egypt, of gathering. But Egypt mean bondage. So ones could not let go of the gold to let in the truth. So they die with their gold and you take the truth and go away. So you go to a place where someone will hear. So Greece accepted much of your teachings. So when you go to Greece again, when you go to Delphi, stand there and remember who you are. This will help you. Each of the lands you go, you will find a piece of the Self. And when the mosaic finish, you are not going to believe what you are. So this going to be exciting thing for you."

"But you will speak to many about saving the Earth. For truly, she is in great agony. So you are going to have to inspire in ones hearts, the desire to make a difference."

"You are in midst of building huge shrine, in the internal world, in the inner world. And this shrine, what is a shrine is when holy things are in a place to lift the hearts of those who have not yet found their own holiness. So you are building this place for ones to come that are frightened and in fear, and you will bring them to this place in meditation, for them to set in this holy place. So you have brought back the crystals from Atlantis. You have brought back the sounds from the American native. And you have brought back the *quiet*, from Egypt. So these things you will give when you bring ones to meet the Self."

"So in your stillness, and we see you still have trouble with this mind being still, it is so active. It just run away," She laughed.

"I don't know what to do."

"Uhh, try to use sound. Listen and let music pull you away. And this begin to quiet the mind. Even if you sit in quiet only for two minutes, you will begin to build to higher. So even for two minutes at a time, it will spread to three and soon you will be able to do this, to make quiet. But your mind has so much to learn, is why it is not quiet. It wants to know more and more and more. As a small child come to this Earth, you wanted to know. You wanted to understand. And you could not get ones to answer. Truly they did not know the answer to the questions you asked, so they tried to make it unimportant, for you would not believe they just did not know."

*

Great changes were taking place in my life. Rather than seeking satisfaction in the external world, I began to find greater rewards in the internal one. A sense of magic was growing and many of the needs that the physical world could once satisfy, became unimportant.

A change in work and my living space resulted. Instead of a larger home, I rented a smaller space that would be more affordable and allow more time for spiritual pursuits.

On my thirty-third birthday, I spontaneously walked outside. Within a large city, the new place offered amazing privacy. A flowing creek was a mere twenty feet from my dining room window. And animals would regularly venture through.

But on this day as I stood outside, I casually looked up to the sky. At first I was a little surprised to see a cloud formation that seemed to resemble the head of a horse. Then on closer inspection, and as the cloud continued to evolve, I realized it didn't just look similar to the head of a horse. *It had turned into a perfectly sculpted horse's head.* Flared nostrils, pricked ears and throat latch all perfectly visible. It was an absolute work of art.

At first I didn't what to do. I considered running inside to get a camera. But fearing that I would miss too much of the experience, I just stood still, absorbed its energy and reflected on its meaning. It only lasted a few more minutes, and then it was gone.

A Conversation

"It is really a burden to have to pull all of this up," I told Mary. With many unexpected memories returning, I was left feeling drained. And I was then slowly remembering a pivotal life, one that had deeply injured me and still limited me today.

"Because there are still ones in Earth that believe this man did not exist. But do you know why? Because he was magic. It is hard to place fingerprint of the magician," She said. "But we see the dream is the same, the desire to give the same—to make a difference the same."

"Does my guide have anything to say to me?"

"Yes, this is a time of the letting go of the sword. This is the time of recognizing that great power came from within, that the ones that you are meeting this time from the past are again challenging you as they did long ago. But if you stay true to you, the outcome will be different."

There was a Long pause.

"See the only thing that happened that ended your reign was you stopped being true to you. When you begin to allow others to decide for you," She added.

"That's a contradiction to all of the information that I've gotten. I was told it was not my fault," I said.

"It was not. And it wasn't fault. It was that you, in your lack of trust in you, you lost you."

"How?" I asked.

"Because you begin to listen too much to the outside. You begin to doubt you. Do you see? So it wasn't the outcome of the world that was different. It was *your* outcome that was different," She answered.

"So if I hadn't of doubted me, I wouldn't have been killed?"

"Right. You wouldn't have been in battle if it were not for that. You wanted to please others."

"But that is what I thought originally, but then I began to get other answers," I added.

"But again, it was the way it was spoken, not what you have received."

But I thought I had received this correctly," I told her.

"Your death changed nothing for the outer world. It changed your life. So you had no fault in this. It is just that you do not have the honor and the joy that you could have had. The world was not different because you died. So that part was not a thing to blame."

"Hmmm," I paused. "I understand how there could be a lot of misinformation."

"Was it your fault? No. Was it your choice? Yes. Because you listened to other forces. You listened to other ones above your own inner guidance—that is why you died."

"Whether you believe it is a bad or a good thing is up to you. Your heart was broken."

"By their deaths?"

"By the death of those you loved. By the ones around you that your heart ached for. And yet you saw though clearly that you were tricked. Do you see? Try to remember, that those around you set up a situation where you would have to harm those you loved. Do you see? Can you remember?" She said, with a long pause.

"And remember the day you realized what they had done. And so, you really died that day. But it was only a matter of time passage before the body left also. But the spirit died with the knowledge it had been betrayed. So did you cause? No. But by not hearing you, by not taking a stand with yourself and your belief you were prepared to die," She paused.

"But you did not cause the world to be the way it was afterward. You could not have changed it if you stayed—because it was a time for change. It was as time prepared. So all of the ones, the magic ones who surrounded you in the great talking, trying to talk you from this, you held, to the knowledge that part of you was gone. And so you followed that part of you beyond."

Mary had disturbed me with what she shared this day. I was barely awakening. Then as if a bomb had been dropped in my lap, I suddenly have to face a tragedy that I cannot even remember. But the memories came, slowly at first, then as if a door had been fully opened. Every few nights, I'd be taken back in time to a new era, lives with success, failures and a similar theme. Often I would establish hope, only to have that hope taken in the end...

An Ancient Past

My life had already changed focus from Earthly pursuits to spiritual ones. But the desire to remember was just beginning to take hold. I wanted to know what my soul had once experienced and I was prepared to make the necessary life changes to bring that into my consciousness. My spiritual practice evolved to include regular intervals of fasting, contemplation and journaling. And my spiritual awareness rapidly expanded. My life continued toward the internal and with that, even more memories came. I had forgotten that day as a child, when I went into my backyard and knelt, sitting down with my feet tucked beneath me.

"Much of your difficulty is about this," I was told.

In the next moment, I saw a chalice appear. Floating from a wooden box, it stood prominently in front of me.

Next, images led me back to a past life in which I had been a spiritual teacher. I could feel powerful feelings emanating from the life.

I had obviously caused much conflict with my assertions about spirituality that many had resisted. In the end, I was put to death, forced to drink poison from the chalice that was now appearing before me.

The thought began to be impressed into my mind, *"This was about the past—not the future."*

Already as a small child, I had become obsessed with being poisoned and had often feared that I would die from poisoning. There were times when I told my father that I was afraid the food we were about to eat was poisoned. I sometimes even had the symptoms of being poisoned, with nausea and vomiting. But the doctors could never find anything wrong.

This was a life for me, where all of my past lives were merging. As if all converging into one melting pot, memories from many lives were slowly pouring into this one, into my present day consciousness.

During the day for much of my life, I worked as a carpenter. It grounded me and provided me with a means to survive in the world, but my nights were different. I gained access to a realm of discovery that most people could not imagine.

These internal pressures demanded that my spiritual practice evolve. When I became anxious, I intuitively learned rather than to perpetuate it with activity, to simply stop and sit in the anxiety. Instead of acting when I felt most desperate—I sat still, forcing myself to become conscious of its source. I would have to ask myself many questions. Where was my fear originating? What triggered these feelings? But with each experience, I learned how to navigate through the desperate state until calm returned. This way, I prevented my fear from manifesting in the Earth's dimension. It prevented me from pacifying the anxiety with activity, simply for the purpose of diffusing my awareness. In doing so, I gained more freedom, less conflict with others, more consciousness and access to greater doors in the dream world...

*

Within a hazy dream, my consciousness began to expand and I found myself staring at what appeared to be a sheet of polished metal hanging on a stone wall. In its reflection, was a face I did not recognize. I could also see in the mirror that I was in a very small room, that there was another stone wall just a few feet behind me.

I had a handsome face, mostly covered by a full beard, and my hair was a light brown color. But to my surprise, I could see that my mustache grew over my lips completely concealing them from view.

My awareness continued to expand and I was no longer in a simple dream—I had become completely conscious. Even though my body was asleep, I was now fully awake in this experience.

"*Ahhhhhhhh,*" I yelled loudly, before doubling over. Feeling the heaviness of the burdens this man carried, I could feel my stomach heave. In an instant, I threw up a ball of baby snakes onto the floor to my side.

"*Uhhh*," I gasped, reaching out with my arm as I stepped back to lean against the wall. Someone appeared to my side.

"*I've got to find a doctor!*," I exclaimed to him, unable to recover from the overwhelming shock.

Very calmly he replied, "You know, I've seen this before. Sometimes you are just completely fine afterward," He insisted.

I took in a couple of deep breaths, "*Ok,*" I yelled.

Looking back into the mirror, I could see that my face was sweating and my moustache wet from throwing up. Trying to regain my composure, I continued to breathe deeply. My mind, thoroughly overwhelmed demanded, "*What I am I doing here?*"

I had the knowledge of my current day self, but I was in the body of another. And I wanted to be experiencing *anything* other than this. How long would I have to endure these desperate feelings? How long would I have to be in this man's body? It was beyond overwhelming.

Seconds passed that seemed like hours. I didn't know what I was waiting for, but I didn't want to continue with this experience. I didn't want to leave this room and continue in this man's life.

I delayed all that I could, but I still remained in this man's body. And it soon became apparent that I was going to have to deal with this, by continuing as this unknown man. As best I could, I mentally prepared myself for whatever I must face and I turned to venture into the rest of the castle. Thankfully, I then lost consciousness…

This experience would stay in the forefront of my mind for months, and perhaps take years to transmute. In my current life, I had worked hard to minimize the strength of my ego. My life itself had actually afforded much work upon my ego, and it didn't have enough density to contain the wound I had suffered as this king. Waking up in that dimension, bearing the full burden of his responsibility—without the same ego, I had to release his pain. His suffering was still limiting me today. But after that experience, it would not have as much power over me, and the resulting purification would enable me to reach the next level in consciousness.

Temptation

As I was now becoming very clairaudient in my psychic perceptions, another challenge was presented. I would often hear a voice encouraging me to make a change in my life. At first it was very insistent, sometimes even demanding, but it was almost always accompanied by a sense of urgency.

"You must act now, there is but a small window of opportunity for this," I'd hear, often upon waking or sometimes in a dream. It was usually a voice without a face, but I would also meet entities in out of body experiences offering similar guidance.

The requests were usually quite benign. Perhaps to go to a certain place, or participate in an event, or to move to another location. And at first, I often followed its urging. But I often found myself doing things that I didn't enjoy.

At the same time, I would have dreams of unlocked doors, doors blown open or somehow otherwise unsecured. It was a very challenging time, as I didn't have enough personal trust in myself to know what I should be doing in any given moment. While I didn't have any trouble with third dimensional beings overpowering my life, I hadn't yet learned how to protect myself from those in the spirit dimension. The power in their voice seemed to dwarf my own, and their dynamic personalities, unfettered by the heaviness of an Earth ego gave them a persuasive edge. I didn't have much of a choice. I had to take the long road, of learning what was safe and what was not, what inspired me and what left me longing. But since my heart was still injured from the past, I couldn't stand in my own power, initially...

A Reading

You must not wrestle with others," Mary laughed. "Because this is not the time, this is not the time."

"I try not to," I replied.

"Sometimes ones just have to get into a different space and not enter. Do you see? You have to see, Earth is not real and their fears are not real. Don't let them pull you into their fears. So it is almost as though, competitiveness that is an ancient thing, is time to be finished—because you have too much to give. And your part is strong because you have built so much energy from the past. So it is very important that you get in balance and go with this and not let biting on the side draw you from your goal. Do you see? Because it is too important a goal. And it has too many ramifications for others, your students. So it is very important that you keep a clear vision and you hold that vision, where they will understand it also. Very important, for in Earth, everyone has different belief system. There are no two the same. But often, by presenting what you have to offer, ones will pick out of it what is their part and then they gather from many sources.

You are just about to make a great leap. And you want to let this, wings happen with this. Let nothing in Earth pull you back. Not the speaking, not the opinion, not the way they present a thing. But that it is important that you see your purpose with God and you let this flow, because all of the things that have created you, all of the things that you have done in the Earth place, to come to today, must now be acknowledged. So you are in time of initiation, so everything harder. It is, because everything clamp down when it is time for initiation. Because that is the test, to say that, 'This is not real, no one can take my good away.' No one can say just who I am or what I am going to accomplish. This is between my God and myself. And that is what that is about. And you are getting it but it is painful, your little heart bleeding. Do you see? Truly, because your emotional body in great pain, because you are hurt deeply and you must not allow that. There will be many that do not understand what you are about, there will be many that do not understand that you have come to make their life easier. So you just give and don't look back to see who receives. And that is very important also. So this is a time before the great activity. This is that breath of air before you have to run so hard. So there will become a time when you look back and think this was wonderful time," She laughed.

"But the dream is opening. It is come up through much mud, like the lotus to bloom. And it is just before the opening," She paused.

"And that is why we asked you to come here to make it easier, to talk with us today. *Don't get discouraged.* It is not as it looks. It is not a mess, it just looks like it. And it looks like ones are resisting and that you are standing alone on a mountain. You are standing on a mountain—*but you are not alone*. There are many unseen people with you. Don't get discouraged, because you are so close to home. Don't do it now," She laughed again.

"The travel is coming soon and this is going to help you to expand."

"Being able to travel?"

"Yes, yes. So all of this is *just* close now. You have worked too hard to allow anything to draw you down now. The energy you must push back up. Say, the whole thing is about God. The whole thing is about goodness and the path they walk, or what they believe, or the wrestling—*means nothing*. The importance is that you begin to recognize the God within you and honor that. So once you truly know that it is there and you feel the expansion of it, nothing outside going to touch you. And then, the dreams will come true."

*

Slowly becoming conscious in an out of body experience, I could see that I was in some sort of fenced compound, not unlike what I might have seen in a movie about Africa. I was making my way toward its center, the total area being perhaps fifty yards across, fence to fence, when my eyes fixated upon a pride of lions carefully watching me.

First a cold chill, then terror coursed through my body. There was no barrier between myself and the lions, and my fear had rung an alarm for them. They immediately jumped up and began to walk toward me.

In a fraction of a second, I looked for an escape. There was a house on one end, a few trees scattered throughout the property, but no safe ground that I could easily reach before becoming dinner. I turned around and began to run back to the gate that I had just walked through, before rising in conscious in this out of body experience. Shifting from being semi-conscious to full consciousness, everything was happening so quickly that I didn't actually know I was out of body. The experience being completely real, I believed I was in great danger.

Looking over my shoulder, I could see that the lions were now running toward me and that there was no way possible for me to reach the gate before they would be upon me. I had no choice. I had to turn and face them.

After turning around, I began slowly walking toward them. I then took in a deep breath of surrender and calmly prepared to meet them. Their demeanor quickly changed.

At the same time, I noticed that I was able to view some sort of concentric lines around each lion, several lines around each one. There were individual lines, and group lines that showed the energy and thoughts of each lion, as an individual and as a group. I also noticed that I could see similar concentric lines around my own body.

All this was absorbed into my mind in just seconds. And somehow, I intuitively knew how to read this information. I could see that the laws of physics were at play, that the lions themselves were bound by spiritual law itself. Their behavior was limited, based upon what was dictated by the concentric lines overlapping their own. In other words, for the lions to be able to harm me, my own concentric lines had to open to theirs in a way to allow it. I had to fear, else I could not be harmed.

With this knowledge, I began to relax, and held out my hand when the first one reached me. As we met and my own lines began to overlap the others, their hostility was instantly transmuted, they quickly calmed down and by the time the entire pride arrived, treated me as if I was one of their own. I touched one to scratch its head as I lost consciousness. Test, apparently passed...

For any aspiring dreamers, do not let this frighten you. This was a test that had been prepared for unconsciously while in travel. And I likely even failed before this conscious attempt. The other world, the place I call home, is a place of energy. Power is developed through experience and these metaphors of animals are merely representative of those powers. It was an energetic test of my ability to manage certain frequencies of thought. It's one of the benefits afforded in the Earth; animals exist to collectively hold the God energy.

When travelling out of body, a portion of one's ego stays in the physical body. So the challenges in alternate dimensions are usually easier than what would be experienced in the physical Earth. We are often lighter in spirit there and not as overwhelmed by experience. And when a dreamer has reached the level of becoming conscious in out of body travel, a portion of that energy is brought into the waking life. Trace energies of the power and emotion discovered there come into the physical body, resulting in a gradual spiritual awakening.

While these experiences are liberating, they can also be a little wearying when experienced on a regular basis. And they break the ego down further in the process.

One evening while doing internal spiritual work, I came across a new level of fear. I didn't understand it, so I casually said a prayer, that some experience might come to me in order to understand, transmute and release it.

After deciding to go out for dinner, I walked outside to get in my truck. It was early evening, a little over an hour before sunset and the nature just outside my door had made that evening shift. It was coming alive again after bearing the heat of the day. With the sun no longer overhead, the trees cast long shadows across the path I was walking.

I got in my truck, started the engine, backed out and was driving along a six lane residential road, in a very developed city when a hawk swooped down from the sky and began to fly with me in my direction of travel. The hawk was on the driver's side of my vehicle, flying parallel with and maybe ten feet off the ground. This was no coincidence—He was looking directly at me.

My mouth dropped open.

At this time in my life, I was very conscious of Native American Animal Medicines and I knew this was important. The hawk continued to fly at the identical speed I was traveling and would occasionally look forward, but mostly stared directly into my eyes, all the while his wings vigorously beat to keep his position.

I had to focus on my own driving, but every few seconds I looked over to him while trying to receive a message. After what seemed like a few minutes, he finally began rising in altitude and disappeared amongst the trees lining the road.

I thought to myself for a moment, then became very disturbed. I still didn't know what this meant, but I did feel it to be a warning, some sort of omen in which I might need spiritual protection. I decided that I would go to the restaurant, eat and quickly return home.

On the return trip...

I had almost forgotten about the Hawk, and was returning home when a car pulled out in front of me. Even though there were three lanes of traffic, an empty lane on either side of me, the driver chose the center lane, causing me to heavily hit my brakes. I slowed from around forty miles an hour to twenty in just a few seconds.

While I did nothing in the physical dimension to offend anyone, no hand gesture, erratic steering, etc., I did feel a lot of anger inside. They must have felt it too, as moments later I could see them pointing back toward me while moving to the inside lane to allow me to pass. While I ignored their rants, I could now hear them yelling at me as my truck began to pass them.

But they weren't going to let this go. It was obvious now that they had been drinking, as their vehicle had difficulty staying within a lane. With both driver and passenger windows rolled down, I could see arms and gestures from both of the occupants.

I really wasn't expecting any more trouble, but I could feel their hostility escalating. When I was forced to stop next to them at a light, the driver got out of his vehicle and came up to my window.

The glass of my truck was heavily smoked, so he probably couldn't see me. But any anxiety I felt about this conflict had passed, as I quickly shifted into a complete surrender.

When I rolled down my window to look him in the eye, I could see a barely conscious soul, heavily inebriated that was now showing a great amount of fear. He had most certainly planned to be violent, but instantly became docile.

"Did you know your tail lights were out?" He asked.

Stunned, I didn't know how to answer. I thought back,

'Were they ever behind me?' If they were, I certainly didn't remember it, and I suddenly felt a little foolish, as if perhaps this encounter was partially my fault.

"No, I didn't realize that," I said, beginning to lose awareness of the situation.

"Yeah, I just wanted to tell you that," He insisted, suddenly seeming personable. "We had to hit our brakes when we were behind you."

He said a few more things, then turned to walk back to his car.

By now, the passenger had become irate, was still yelling and opened the door to get out. The driver, a much bigger man, picked him up and literally threw him back into the car as the light turned green. I drove off while trying to figure out what had just happened.

After a lot of review and even a check of my taillights, I realized they had never been behind me. I don't know where that story came from, but it was a way to end the confrontation peacefully. I was thankful that it was so easily neutralized, but it would sit on my mind for days.

How did that happen and why? Of course I can't say for certain, but I learned to be more careful about requests of the Universe. It was an answer to the casual prayer, a prayer to help me release fear.

Initiation

"There are so many things that we are not allowed to tell you because of where you are in your growth. Once you go through the initiation we can tell you more. But now, so much is built in your faith in self and in your purpose for being. Once you make this leap in faith, then we can talk about it. But you are going to go into this test momentarily, so we can't give you answer," Mary began.

"This isn't even the test yet!" I laughed.

Joining my laughter, she added, "This is the test but, initiation comes as result of this testing. Part of the test for you to trust what you receive directly from God, do you see? Not from teachers and not even from us, unless it correspond to your heart. If it correspond to your heart, then you know it is real."

I looked confused.

"We have brought you here to shake you up."

"I'm used to it now," I mused.

"But also to tell you it is the initiation, and that is why you have to keep going back to you. *What do I believe? What do I feel? What do I think? What do I know?* You must say," She paused.

"There are people in Earth on levels of expression, learning all kind of things, each for the area that they will teach. So this does not match this, but both can be so. You see? There are those that are suppose to learn through the Earth. So they will learn through relationships, they will learn how to speak this, or how not to do this, or how to give, how to serve. There are those who came to bring great knowledge and to stack that, for others to use later. There are those that are coming to understand things way from here, distance from here, philosophy from here, and those will teach those. So there are all kind of levels."

"So don't waste your energy wrestling with someone else. Don't waste your energy. Accept what you know from the past, what it is you brought forward. And that is the only reason to know the past. Because you will see, this power is in me today. This power is in me today. My capacity for magic is in me today. Because you are always going to go higher. You are not going to be higher and then go down. So no matter what you believe you are more powerful today than ever before."

"Right now?" I asked.

"*Absolutely*. Now you have to just remember where you have left this power. You have the capacity this day to do greater things than you have ever done. These are all waiting for your awakening. So, it is not that you have to produce it. It is already in existence. But you have been so busy looking back that you have not seen what is here. So now, the next step is to see that it is here, to see what you are capable of today and to not let anything distract you from your purpose. You have come to make a difference in great numbers of people. So you have to believe in you to do this. And you can't compare because you are not like anyone else in Earth. So it is almost as though this ancient brother and you are challenging each other to see who can be fastest. (Speaking about a friend and ancient adversary currently in my life.) It does not matter how fast, the importance is that the world is changed when you are finished. So that is what you ones are all about, that is what you are doing. You are drawing ones that have known you in many lifetimes. Some you have known because you have wrestled with them. Some come into a life because you were friends together. So you are building up both. But a part of you is still standing above, watching from a distance. You are still having trouble letting ones love you. So your loneliness is not because they do not want to be near you, but there is still a part that is afraid to let them too near. Do you see? There is still a part of you that is shy. And that is not bad, it is the sensitive part of you. The other part is going to do what it has come to do. So, trust in that part. But the stress, all this neck and shoulder, the wanting the perfect so badly that you punish you everyday, is not how you are going to get what you want. It is by praise and love that this is going to happen," She finished.

*

With my physical body sound asleep, I awoke to see beams of light coming from the ceiling. Though my body remained asleep—I had become completely conscious within this dream experience. I was aware of what was happening in the dimension just above the physical Earth.

I had not *heard* light before this, but it definitely had a sound, not too different than what might be heard on an episode of Star Trek, when people were being beamed onto the ship.

The beams were initially directed at my feet. And the light hitting me caused feelings similar to being in a Jacuzzi, with bubbles flowing around my body. But in this instance, the bubbles were completely contained, *within* my body. It was as if the light was transmuting darkness within my soul, and as it was released, turned into bubbles. With the beams moving slowly up my body, they continually caused the release of more bubbles. Following the natural flow of energy, the bubbles moved upward and out of my head. Whatever energy that had been transmuted by the light was gone from my body in a few seconds.

I would often remember this experience, witnessing the body's energy flow and how it released darkness. I realized that this was an ongoing process of transmutation that would in time, render the ability to have a dramatically increased consciousness.

*

I had experienced dozens of out of body travels by now, and there was often a very unique element to each one. The world outside the physical Earth, in the dream world, was very different than my awake life. It was a world of energy, symbolism, and consequence. While it seemed like there were not always repercussions for every action when we are awake, I was learning that indeed there was. And beyond just negative consequence, there would also be actions to lift one up. If someone was aspiring to raise their awareness and become more conscious of God, there would be great efforts from the Universe to uplift that soul...

Whale Medicine

Some indigenous cultures believe the whale to embody the vibration of remembrance, the remembering of the eternal Self. I remember Mary mentioning the whale once, in our monthly Group Gathering, saying something to the effect, "Man would like to think that he is the most evolved species on the planet, when he is not."

And once in a dream experience, in February 1996, I was told that a gray whale of great importance had died, that was so powerful that he would be deeply missed. While hearing this, I began to envision a whale that actually influenced the calm of the entire planet. I also saw the emanations of his song extending through the water, the land and beyond. It seemed as though his voice completely saturated the Earth, even traveling out into space.

But I had no idea that a more direct encounter was imminent. When waking up—fully conscious—in the mouth of whale, I only had one thought,

"That poor bastard Jonah—I guess this really can happen!"

Then my mind focused on the task at hand, *"What am I doing here?!!"*

I was almost getting used to finding myself in these situations, but the experiences seemed to be growing in difficulty. In this state, I was not thinking, 'It's ok, I am in an out of body experience.' The state of being I was experiencing would be the same if I had actually been in a whale. I had to deal with the situation as if it were real.

I wanted out! I had to get out and do so as fast as I could. I crawled over on my knees to the whale's lip and lifted upward.

Although the experience was as real as it could be, there were obviously other forces at play. When I looked out, no water entered. Instead, I could actually see sky and open sea. There was no land in site.

It quickly felt more dangerous to leave than stay, so I returned to where I had been sitting in the back of the whale's mouth. It wasn't far to crawl. From back to front, the distance was ten to twelve feet. I sat and considered my options.

While I was initially ready to jump out and make the best of it, it became apparent I would drown. Swimming for it was obviously not the best option. I was truly paralyzed. There was nothing to do but wait.

I looked at the interior of his mouth in wonder, inhaling the salty air while hearing the heavy breathing from this giant. Along with the ocean sounds and sloshing water, my senses were otherwise denied of experience. I was good for a few minutes, but as the fear overpowered me, I lost consciousness.

There were many things to learn from this most recent travel. For one, I was confused about my life, about which direction to take. This seemed to be a subtle suggestion, or perhaps a dramatic insistence that I should just stay where I was in my life and not make any changes. Also, there is the magnetic energy of a whale that triggers memory, past life memory, returning eternal wisdom and knowledge. And my memories from the past were most certainly returning, and in the future perhaps with the help of this experience.

A Past in Spain

"One of the things, I don't know if you've remembered, but I have a sense that you were…that you died in a concentration camp, in your last life," Carla told me.

"In my *last* life?" I answered.

"Uh huh, could that be true? Because I have seen you, two or three times now in a vision, caged. So I have wondered about that. So what I can see, is only from here up," She said, motioning from the waist up with her hand. "But what I can see is the lines of the cage. I would say a cage rather than a cell."

"Yes, I was in a cage once," I admitted.

"And you were in a brown…all I can tell is its brown, it looks almost burlappy."

"I woke up from a dream once, repeating over and over, 'six is hate, six is hate'," I told her. "I was going to ask Mary about that. I believe I was in prison for six years. And then I had my head cut off. But it was like a cage that I was in."

"Yes, it looks like a cage," She agreed.

"It's a cage in a room. Is that what you are seeing?"

"Uh huh, yes."

"I was going to ask her today about it."

"So you are remembering all of this for a reason. It's a really important reason to remember all of this," She pressed. "Part of it is so you can learn patterns and not get caught in them again."

"That's why they have to tell you what you have done, to get a different sense of yourself. And maybe why you were in the cage is because you had too much power then, is why they did that," She added.

"I am afraid of being killed or being captured."

"Usually you won't have the same thing happen to you again. So they aren't going to kill you this time. They might pressure you. But in the end, if someone stays steady on their course, no one can hurt them, no matter what they say about them. You see that every day."

Moments later, Carla began her prayer, left her body and Mary began speaking through her,

"Again, it is correct what this body I wear speak, you are gaining power from the past, to use in the now. To battle with sword – *Not* who you are today. You are going to battle with love, with caring, with support, with words."

"The number came to me in a dream, I once awoke saying '57926' over and over and later in the night, 'six is hate'," I stated.

Her tone turned solemn and she hesitated before replying, "This was a time, was made for you in Spain, on your hand," She said, pointing to the back of her left hand with her right finger.

"Six is hate?"

"Yes, yes," She paused. "You offended, very powerful king. And then wouldn't shut up. He kept saying, '*Don't say anymore.*' So you spoke again. So you finally end up to be punished. And put to death eventually."

Is that when I was in that cage that Carla was talking about?"

"Yes."

"I was in there for six years?"

"Yes, yes. And even there, you did not stop speaking. You inspired people from there. So, you have great courage. Because it would have been much simpler to let people think what they wished and for you to be released. Because you kept being told, if you would just shut up, you would be released. Ones would gather and you would speak even being held away from the window by a cage in the center."

"I can see all of that."

"Yes. So you would speak loud so they would hear you. So eventually they put you to death, to stop you from speaking. But ones had already taken courage from you. So they did not stop you in time to stop you truly."

Carla's Work

Carla had her own challenges. I expect that she had similar dream experiences to my own, but in addition to that, there were some additional physical issues to face.

I am certain that Carla has trained in many past lives to perfect her Mediumship, and that has left her open in a way that most others can't really imagine. For one, Mary could accidentally pop in unannounced. I don't think it happened often, but Mary had been known to make purchases on Carla's behalf when on shopping trips. When a chipmunk telephone was purchased without Carla's memory, she had to rethink things. And then there was a lamp that appeared in her home. After a couple of days she said to her husband, "That is the ugliest lamp. Where did it come from?"

"You bought it," he replied.

It was likely about that time when Carla stopped driving. It was just too risky to have Mary unexpectedly behind the wheel.

In a conversation with Carla, she told me,

"I had a near death experience at fifteen. And I also was told at thirty-three my life would change. And thirty-three has shown up in my life continually since I was fifteen. And at thirty-three I went in trance," She said.

"One of the things they've learned is when someone goes into trance the way I do, it's not good for the physical body anymore. They…were learning that…not that it injures the body but it is a very strong energy and you go from this very high level back into this, like you womp into concrete," She added.

"Oh," I replied.

"But what they are going to do, is more and more they are going to have people in an altered state. But you won't be totally unconscious. And they found this was easier on the physical body. So what you will have to do is repeat the words or, they will come right through you. But they will put them right in you. They call it brain impress. So they put the thoughts in you and they come out of you, almost like you were doing it. And so I have friends that do it this way. When I go into trance, I just see the white cross and follow it."

"But everything that has happened to you has made you powerful and given you the strength to be what you are going to be. And you will see that the very personal things that have happened to you will be shared with someone else."

"It's just amazing that there's no wasted time. You'll find that things that happened to you as a child, that maybe you didn't remember until you start to talk, you see why they happened. Because you needed that information to talk with this group over here or this group over here. And people listen more when someone else has been there. And see that's the thing. I have been through just about everything there is."

"Pretty soon you'll find out that you can't even hold a judgment. It's just wonderful. Because I don't know about your family, but I was raised to be judgmental," Carla laughed.

"To say that's wrong and that's right. You be amazed in working with a guide in a short time that you can't judge because you'll know that everything has purpose. Pretty soon you'll say 'gosh I wish they didn't have to go through that to get there' but know that there is a good reason and the people are wonderful. They are beautiful. So pretty soon there is no separation. And that's what the guides are teaching very strongly right now that there is no separation in people. We are all here looking for the same things. Each with a gift to give that helps to bring that about."

"So particularly since I had that last near death experience, I came back with a more universal vision. There is something I saw that I don't remember, but made me see that whole world. Because in my work, I just work with individuals...even in a group...with that individual soul to be able to express everything that they are. Now I still have that vision, but now I see them as team players. They're not going to be loners anymore. So that's going to be good."

"Because y'all are doing things now that we haven't done since probably Atlantis." She finished.

*

By now ability to travel the dimensions was at a peak. Having perhaps seven to ten overwhelmingly powerful travels a week took the largest portion of my energy. During the daytime, about half my thoughts weren't about my physical life—they were about my dreamtime travels.

It had taken several years of purification work to reach this level, with having made my spiritual work my life's priority. But I didn't realize that the consciousness of the planet was going to decline.

I was living in a major metropolitan area at the time, the downtown skyline within view of home. And it wasn't the safest part of town—I could hear gunshots being fired nightly. So the spiritual vibration of the place was already challenging, and the resulting desperation created from the violence, negatively grounded me. My dream travels stopped the day the U.S. invaded Iraq. Plunging the planet into a darkened state, my level of purity was no longer high enough to remain fully conscious in the dream state.

While I continued to have a low level consciousness of my dream world, I actually went three months without a single *super* conscious experience. This required me to increase my spiritual purification work so that I might regain a lucid consciousness in those realms.

With the vibration of the Earth dramatically lower, I could feel my own sense of desperation increasing. And I could feel it in those around me as well. One day when driving home from a day of work, I made a right turn from a right turn *also* lane. The person to my right was in a right turn *only* lane.

Believing that I was cutting him off, the driver became enraged and began to follow me, his truck coming within a few feet of my rear bumper. He then pulled beside me, raising his fist, and appeared to be yelling. I ignored him.

But his anger was not letting up and he began to move into my lane, trying to force me off the road. He next pulled in front of me, in an attempt to cut me off—all the while dozens of other cars were around us on this six lane residential thoroughfare.

Now, I was feeling threatened. I pulled out my cell phone to dial 911. Seeing my phone, his eyes widened and he instantly stopped his aggressions. He moved into the next lane and within a couple of minutes, I could no longer see his vehicle. I was tired, ready to get home and just didn't want to pursue it further.

But I was very surprised that evening, when in the dream state, I had to attend his arraignment in court. I've often heard people say, "Let God handle it." But I didn't think it was a literal thing because I didn't know how the spirit world managed all the wrongs in our world. I had assumed that someone wouldn't have to face their failures until the end of their life, but in this court I discovered that I was wrong. Every action is seen and no crime goes unnoticed.

I didn't stay conscious throughout the proceedings, but this man had to face the consequences of his actions. He may have lost a degree of power and been forced to live with a little less consciousness in his daily life, to help him cope. Or perhaps a promotion or something that was about to enter his life was denied. But this incident didn't go without consequence—our failures must be faced. It's really the only way to keep behavior in check.

*

When I was about six years old, several of the other kids on the block had congregated in my driveway. We were all on our bikes, about to ride around the neighborhood when the subject of airplanes came up.

"I was a pilot," I told them. "I flew a Lone Wulf airplane."

A few of them began snickering.

"Not in this life, in my last one," I added for clarification.

Of course this brought even more laughter, leaving me feeling rather silly.

"You didn't live before this life," Someone stated. "You were just born a few years ago."

Past lives had come up on more than one occasion, and each time they did, I was left feeling completely ridiculous. With those kinds of feelings, it didn't take long for the memories to start evaporating.

But it was Mary that once again reminded me, decades later.

"You die in your last life. You were very young. You were a pilot," She said.

"I flew airplanes?"

"Yes, in the war. One regret you had was that you didn't leave anyone behind, breathing, walking, no children. And you were just beginning to attract the womens in your uniform, when you die."

"What happened?" I asked.

"A bomb, was placed to explode upon take-off," She answered.

"I was killed, by my own people?"

"Yes. But you loved the air before that. You were *cocky*," She laughed.

I would later learn more about this life. There had been an incident where I had been flying alone. I had come upon an American Bomber, badly damaged and barely able to maintain altitude. The crew was just trying to get back home. Maneuvering up to their side, I could actually see their faces. But unable to finish them off, I tipped my wings and returned home.

"Why? Why would my own people kill me?" I asked.

"To stop you," Mary answered.

It was never intended to be a long life, nor an inspiring one. But that life offered a direct view of the dark masculine wound. By witnessing the complete absence of the Divine Feminine, I was turned around to face the light. And the life ended any remaining belief in war from within my soul.

Carla's Departure

I didn't feel the need to see Carla, but I couldn't stop considering it. But as each day passed, I would reconsider, "Is it time?"

Finally giving in, I called. Her daughter-in-law answered the phone. I told her that I wanted to schedule an appointment with Carla.

There was a moment of silence, and then an answer, "I am sorry, but Carla passed away the day before yesterday. Her funeral is tomorrow."

Instantly numb, I can barely remember anything else that I said. I do recall acknowledging that I recognized her voice, that I'd seen her often at the gatherings. She remembered me. But the phone call only lasted a few minutes, I got the information about attending the funeral, said goodbye and hung up the phone.

I wailed for hours, cried for days.

I knew she was sick, had even been preparing myself for this. But the last time I saw her, she looked so well, having dramatically recovered from an earlier illness.

Carla gave her Eulogy at the service. It had been a prerecorded message intended for the family, but they decided to share it with everyone. She talked about death, how she could tell that she was dying by watching the faces of those around her. I am sure I had contributed to her realization when once seeing her for a reading. She looked much too ill to be working, yet she continued, seemingly without regard for herself.

I didn't know how to face this. No doubt, my greatest ally had left the Earth and I felt very alone. I would have never allowed all the magic and inspiration to enter my life, had she not been there to encourage it.

But with all of the hope that she had given to so many, she died from an asthma attack. It just didn't seem right to me, that she would have to leave on terms other than her own. And this passage would cause much internal struggle for me. I had to understand why she did not have a peaceful passing...

A Divine Father

I awoke to find myself in the spiritual home of a friend that was once my teacher. When I say spiritual home, I mean the place in which he is from, his true home, where he lives when not incarnated into the physical Earth.

A home beyond anything that I had imagined, I would describe it as something that might resemble a commune or an intentional community today. The patriarch, my friend's spiritual father, oversaw the day to day functions of the place, while always taking time to give any needed emotional support to the members of his family. What this man embodied, is not yet an archetype that is within the Earth's written memory.

While I could easily see that my friend was truly blessed, his conscious mind still had an antagonistic relationship with the father archetype in his waking life. In fact, he had a rather strong hatred for the patriarchal figure in the Earth, while in reality actually having the ideal father. With his deepest soul remembering this man, while his conscious mind had no knowledge of him, an intense longing for reconnection was fueled, that eventually turned into anger and even hatred. Though my friend was an amazing man himself, he was just was unable to cope on a day to day basis without having the conscious blessing his father in spirit offered.

Standing in front of the father, he realized that I had reached consciousness within this experience and nodded his head toward a man sitting on a log in the distance. There was my friend. With his energy emotionally withdrawn, he just stared at the ground before him.

Looking back to the father, I could feel his sadness and see in his face a wealth of compassion for his son, but also a hope that was so strong that I couldn't doubt its resolve. I knew he would do whatever he could to pull his son beyond his despair.

While in the physical Earth, my friend's existence was very minimal. He was barely surviving and had a great resistance to any authority figure. Although he did not create any discord in the world and behaved within the law, the anger that perhaps stemmed from the temporary loss of this amazing father, placed great limits on his life.

It seemed that most of the family members were there in their fullness and were not incarnated into any other realms. Only a few were incarnated in the Earth. Even so, each night, everyone always returned. Or perhaps they had unconscious fragments that never left. But the family unit was always able to connect and offer support to each other.

Even though he had absolutely no knowledge of these experiences, he in fact spent a great amount of time with his *real* family. But there, he was able to receive on a different level and find comfort in a way that could one day help him to thrive in the Earth.

Oneness with the Divine

At some point, one might come to the conclusion that our world is missing a most important facet—the presence of the Divine Feminine—an *essential* element for the world to achieve balance.

What is the dark masculine? I don't know how one can truly identify its presence, but it is easy to find evidence of its existence. I would suggest that it exists within us all in varying degrees—that part of us that believes we can solve every problem with a physical action. It's an impatient part that would deny the ebb and flow of nature and resists allowing us to find harmony with each other and the Earth.

This seems to create an endless accumulation of problems, as an attempt to solve one difficulty creates another. Many people today long for a more holistic approach to life, a natural way that patiently allows for vision and guidance to come from higher realms. This feminine principle of life, where solutions are contemplated and considerations are made for the good of all, comes with the most valuable result. Divine encounters are the result of reaching an internal balance, where we are able to enter a timeless state. As of course it is a sense of timelessness that allows us to enter a dimension that exists outside the constraints of time.

On the surface, it might appear an easy thing to do, to will oneself into inaction. But most have felt that lower pull, that self assuring feeling that says now is the time to act. And in many cases it could very well be correct. But there is a way to neutralize any potential negative energy related to our actions before acting. And that involves a period of self reflection.

I do not trust an external voice, whether from a physical being or one in the spirit world. While either guidance might be good, it may also be influenced by the fear within the soul sharing with me. And while I am often willing to listen to others, I know that the guidance must come from within, else it be tainted by another's ego. The voice of God can only be from within.

When I am considering any life change, or in fact during most decision making, I wait for the presence of the Divine Feminine to enter. While I might be able to make a good decision on my own, in the moment, I often choose to wait. I want the blessing that comes as the masculine and feminine energy find a balance within. Then, I know that my choice is more likely to be supported by the Universe.

*

Still struggling to understand Carla's passing, I awoke within a dream experience. Quite lucid, I found myself seated in a hall in which Carla often spoke. I looked around to see that I was alone. Feeling a little disappointed, my eyes continued to scan the room as I wondered, "Why am I here?"

But I could hear someone speaking to me from the internal plane. They were telling me about a person that worked very hard and didn't take enough time for themselves. Even though many encouraged rest, this anonymous person pressed on with work. The description continued for a couple of minutes—until I turned to my left.

Carla, now seated alone held her hand in the air as her fingers waved self consciously to me. Hair spiked and wearing fashionable dress for the day, she was very attractive and much younger than when she had passed. But the look on her face, tinged with guilt, explained our meeting. She was here to acknowledge that she had lived her life, at least in the end, without balance. There was no need for words. I quickly awoke.

I would have the next several years to consider this meeting. My life course had dramatically changed after meeting Carla. And while I always left a conversation with Mary inspired, I was never really able to balance myself in the world during the time I knew her. I always felt the need to do more than my actual capacity would allow. Mary's vision for me was beyond my capability to produce. And that left me feeling weakened.

The more I thought about Carla, the more I found her departure less and less acceptable. Had she been able to truly embody the wisdom that came through her, she should have been able to live with a reasonable degree of health. And I don't believe her spiritual practice was lacking. She spent a great amount of time in contemplation and journaled on a daily basis. She certainly did not lack discipline. But it would take me a few more years to see what really had led to the health issues she faced. It was the depth of her giving that had always been suspect to me.

Eventually, I would have to accept. Like so many spiritual teachers that begin with great aspirations and good intentions, somewhere along the way she became more attached to what was happening in the outer world, than what was happening in her inner one. While this can bring failure in many endeavors, it is absolute death to the Mystic. The liberation provided by a spiritual life is based on one remaining internally focused, to be slightly more aware of the internal life, than the external one. It's how the world evolves, how God is able to bring spiritual evolution to the Earth plane. But when we become more externally focused, we limit that influence. We become victim of the predominant energy and beliefs in our environment.

It isn't the first time someone with a refined soul has allowed the Earth illusions to influence them. And while Carla did stay very close to her inner world, I believe she was caught by the energy of the illusion.

Never be satisfied, Don't give up, Always want more.

And while she may have lived her personal life without falling victim to these messages, she did give more to the world than she had to give. She worked tirelessly offering teaching to those desperate souls in need of encouragement. She fell into the belief of the Dark Masculine – *Act Now before it's too late*, preventing the Divine Feminine from fully manifesting within her physical body. And because of that, I believe we lost her before her time...

Divine Presence

I awoke to find myself in a Sanctuary. Not unlike a religious place of worship, but this hall didn't seem to have a specific affiliation.

As I was walking through, accompanied by an unknown man, I noticed a beautiful golden glow emanating throughout. It was relatively dim inside, but the interior was washed with the most amazing golden hues, the beams entering from the back of the space. The comforting glow that was placing me in a state of calm, shown through a large transom above two doors in the back wall.

Immediately drawn to them, I felt compelled to see the source of this wondrous light. Opening the doors, I walked out into what was an alcove, exterior walls of windows and vaulted ceiling that created a room outside the large doors. The alcove walls were almost completely glass, though covered with sheets of smoke tinted vellum. The tint dramatically limited the amount of light that could enter, but was still creating this most soothing glow that was magically filling the Sanctuary.

With so much glass, much more light could have been allowed to enter. But this was the correct amount of light, the perfect amount to influence my soul. Standing in its frequency, I could feel balance.

Appreciation

All of those dreams I had experienced throughout the years, seeing visions of open doors, unlocked, and unsecured passages was now coming to an end. I wasn't always vulnerable, but too often I had been misled. Somehow I had exposed my spiritual vibration to something that put me at risk. It was the dominating belief in the Earth—that there is never enough. We always need more. These simple beliefs were corrupting my soul and preventing me from receiving the deepest and greatest satisfaction. For when I finally tired of looking for something else, something more…when I finally believed that I had enough—I was blessed with appreciation. Appreciation, the greatest protection one can have from darkness, finally entered into my life.

Appreciation and Satisfaction, was now offering me a new life experience, a new reference to receive goodness, hope and balance from and in the Earth. I'd come full circle now, and a greater level of hope was now a reality.

Psychic Law

For every action, there is an equal and opposite reaction.

This spiritual law gives us great insight into how the Universe works, for if we are to stand in any polar end of the spectrum, we are attracting the energy from the opposite end. If we adopt an extreme view point, whether liberal or conservative, we are magnetizing thought from the opposite pole to achieve balance. We cannot attach to an extreme and be in absolute truth. We need the opposite frequency to achieve balance.

This may be unpalatable for many to receive. And of course great battles have been fought because of such resistance.

But in the eyes of the spiritual master, the Universe was purposely designed in order to compensate for extreme thought. Saints and Mystics know that to master this dimension, a releasing of the Earth's heaviness is required. That is, releasing beliefs that cause one to magnetize conflict.

You might then say, 'how can I protect myself and those around me if I am unwilling to accept conflict?' But there is a difference in adopting an extreme and protecting the Self. You stand squarely balanced in the Earth when you seek to protect. It is when we cross that line, go beyond protection and enter into the space of our adversary that we attract unnecessary conflict. We can protect ourselves with all our being and remain in balance. It is when we go after another's belief that we create an unstable environment.

And it's really not necessary to force others to adopt our beliefs. For if we are in *Truth* and are able to deeply accept our position, those outside will eventually adopt it as well. This is spiritual law and how the Universe is designed to evolve.

But because of the weakened state of the Earth's collective consciousness, many people are unable to access the inner worlds, the worlds inside of ourselves. And this is a very vulnerable position. In this state, we are unable to be aware of the vast Universe beyond the physical, the place where dreams are inspired and breathed into the Earth's consciousness. We are not conscious that we are receiving guidance and that there is a vast network in these unconscious realms working to bring shifts in awareness as the people of the Earth are ready to receive.

And all that is necessary for this to occur, is that we become open to receive. For when the people of the Earth are truly ready for this change in consciousness, there is no outside force that will be able to stop it from happening.

Prayer, humility and a sincere desire for peace and goodness do not go unanswered. Individually, such desire is answered through an easing of the personal pressures upon an individual. Collectively, it is answered with dramatic shifts in global consciousness. And every time One opens to receive, it is a catalyst for another—So One person truly can make a difference. It is how this change in consciousness has already begun, and how it will progress to completion.

Learning to own your own darkness affords the

Greatest Liberation

For those Dreamers Learning to Communicate with Spirit

One of the most confusing aspects of out of body travel, receiving messages from entities in higher realms can prove very disorienting. While their words may be of the highest truth, they can be spoken from a dimension far above our own, and because of this their messages sometimes require translation.

When first experiencing out of body travel, it's easy to confuse a less evolved soul with someone of a higher evolution. Because an entity in spirit does not have to carry an ego of the same density that is required in the Earth, a very young soul can appear quite dynamic and evolved in an out of body experience. So it does take time to learn to differentiate between the two.

The most evolved beings seldom, if ever, give definitive directions or suggest a specific course of action for your life. The highest beings can inspire you with the simplest of words, as their refined emotions actually have the power to lift you into a higher state of consciousness. On the other hand, less evolved beings—however well intentioned—do not have that capacity and often can only advise you of a specific action to take, something *they* might believe to be beneficial to your life. While there is purpose in both of these interactions, it's very important to realize that anyone simply telling you what to do—is not highly evolved. I always use caution in dealing with such souls.

In the highest dimensions, far above the Earth in vibrational frequency, fear cannot exist as we know it. And it is in these inspirational realms where the energy is created that breathes life into the Earth, into the dreams and thoughts of those incarnated in this world.

We can have our own resistance to these higher frequencies, unconscious fear that separates us from something we wish to manifest or express. We could return to the guidance we were given and claim it to be false. But what is missing from the message, is acknowledgement of the required path we must first walk – life experience that teaches us that certain beliefs, behaviors and attachments we embody might be limiting us. There may be many life experiences between message and manifestation, events that cause us to release beliefs that stand in the way of our longing. It is often a leap in consciousness which ushers in a new aspect of life.

Wanting to immediately manifest a vision, I sometimes find that the Earth refuses to yield. Of course this is actually the purpose of incarnating into a dimension of such density. We are forced to renounce and release those beliefs that prevent us from more deeply aligning with our Higher Power and deepest Self. We may feel the longing to reclaim missing pieces of our soul and we feel the pressure to gain understanding. If we are spiritually focused, we may intuitively realize that we are being asked to release. If we are deeply grounded in the illusion of the Earth, we might suffer through the breaking down of the ego.

I've learned not to attach to the grand visions within my dreams, out of body travel and sight. I've learned if they are meant to arrive in the physical realm, they will arrive in their appropriate time. As it must be, the Earth requires us to cleanse our hearts before we may evolve our experience of oneness, and that seems to be an ongoing evolution into greater depth.

Recommended Reading:

The New Mediumship, by Grace Cooke.

All Works by White Eagle, as channeled by Grace Cooke. Published by The White Eagle Publishing Trust.

Works by Carla Neff Gordan.

To learn more about dreaming, visit the Author's website at

www.consciousdreaming.org

To learn more about Carla and Mary, visit:

www.carlaneffgordan.com

About the Author

Although raised in the city, John Stone was introduced to the outdoors as a young child and often enjoys spending creative time, walking amongst the life-giving trees of the forest. It is there where he finds the inspiration for his writing. Citing two of his greatest life influences as an apprenticeship to a female Shaman and an eleven-year study with spiritualist/medium, the late Carla Neff Gordan, he spends his spare time communing with the Divine and teaching visionary dreaming.

About the Book

In Cultivating the Divine, John Stone takes us on a journey of spiritual discovery with his spiritual teacher and medium, during her life in the Earth and after her death. Learning to receive visions and communications from the higher worlds, he discovers a door into the dream world revealing a world beyond imagination.

A life spent seeking Oneness with God, this is a story of living by Divine Guidance.

Printed in Great Britain
by Amazon